Helping My Dad

Teacher's
Choice
Series

Nancy Lambrecht
Fairfield, California

Illustrations by
Catherine Ward

🔧 **Dominie Press, Inc.**

I help my Dad wash his car.

He helps me wash my bike.

I help my Dad sweep the floor.

He helps me sweep my wagon.

I help my Dad water the grass.

He helps me water my plant.

I help my Dad paint the fence.

He helps me paint my dog's house.

I help my Dad pile the wood.

He helps me pile my blocks.

I help my Dad cook the chicken.

My Dad helps me cook my hot dog.

My Dad and I like to help each other.

About the Author

Nancy Lambrecht completed her educational training at California State University, Sacramento. She has been teaching in Fairfield, California for twenty years. A native Californian, Nancy enjoys reading and collecting children's literature.

All authors' royalties from the sale of the *Teacher's Choice Series* will be used to support various early literacy projects throughout the United States.

Publisher:	Raymond Yuen
Editor:	Bob Rowland
Designer:	Jon Reily
Series Editor:	Stanley L. Swartz
Illustrator:	Catherine Ward

Published by:

🇩 Dominie Press, Inc.

1949 Kellogg Avenue
Carlsbad, California 92008 USA

ISBN 0-7685-0115-6
Printed in Singapore by PH Productions Pte. Ltd.
1 2 3 4 5 6 IP 00 99 98